FLOWER MANDALAS

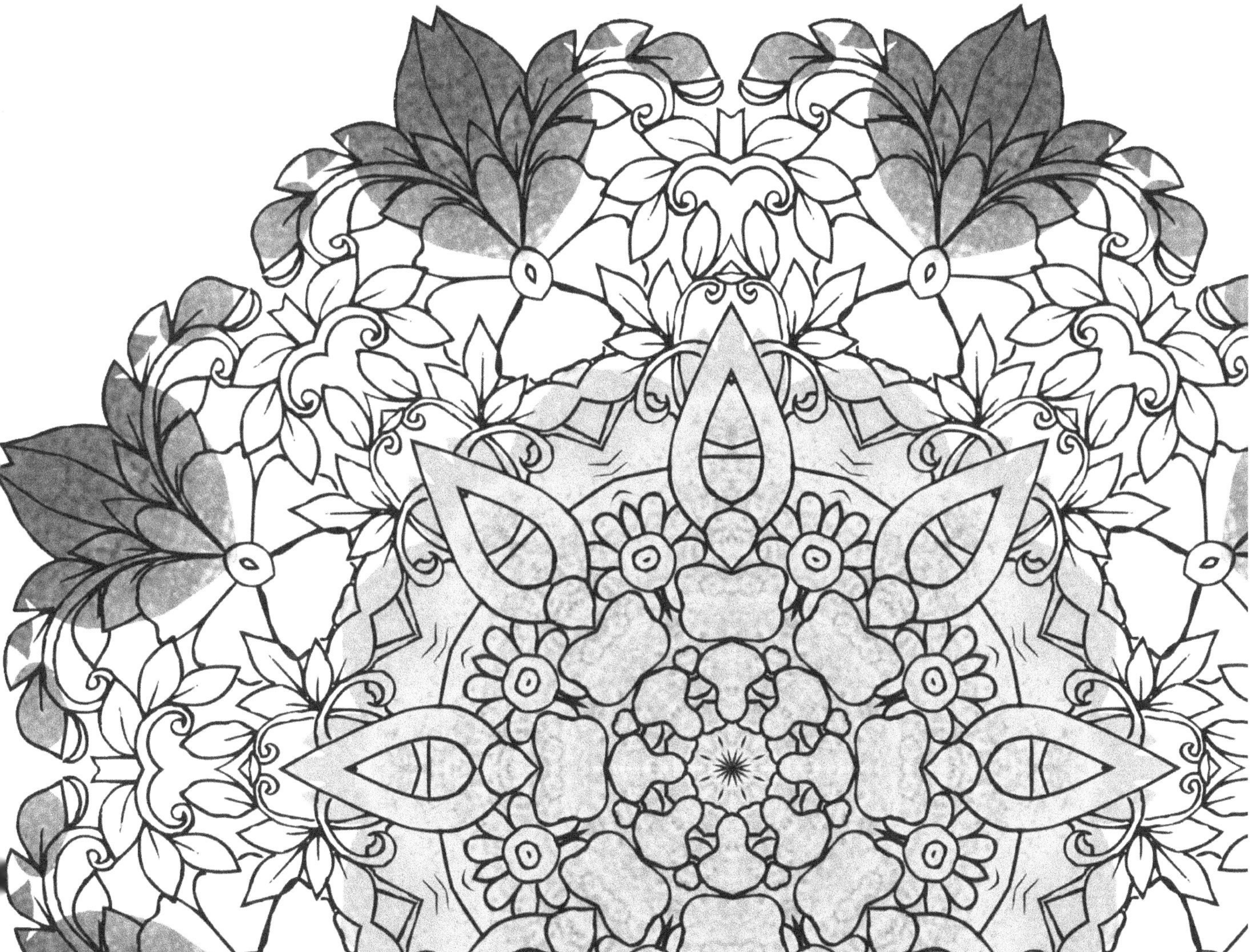

A STRESS RELIEF COLORING BOOK

Vol.3

COLOR TEST PAGE

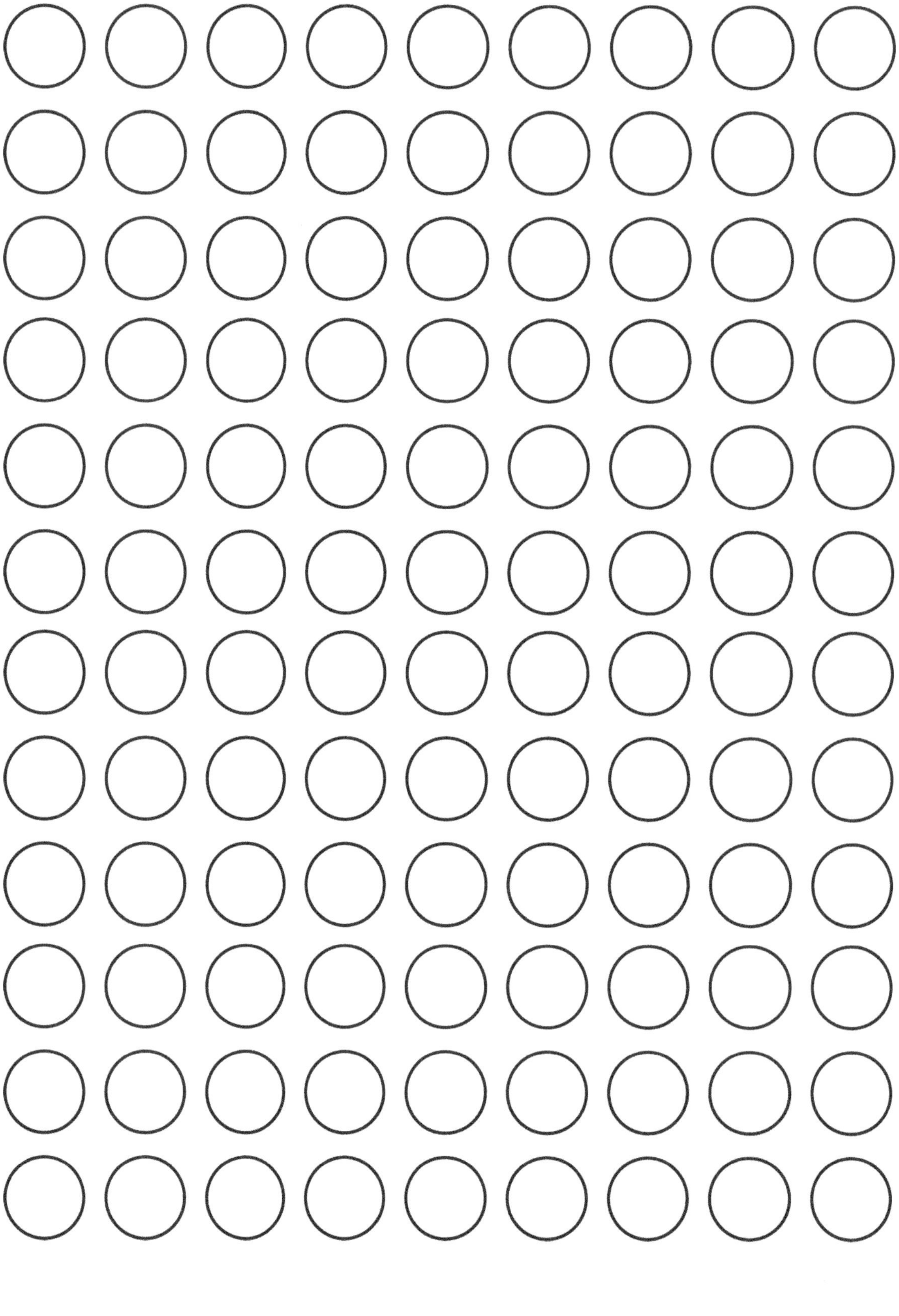

COLOR TEST PAGE

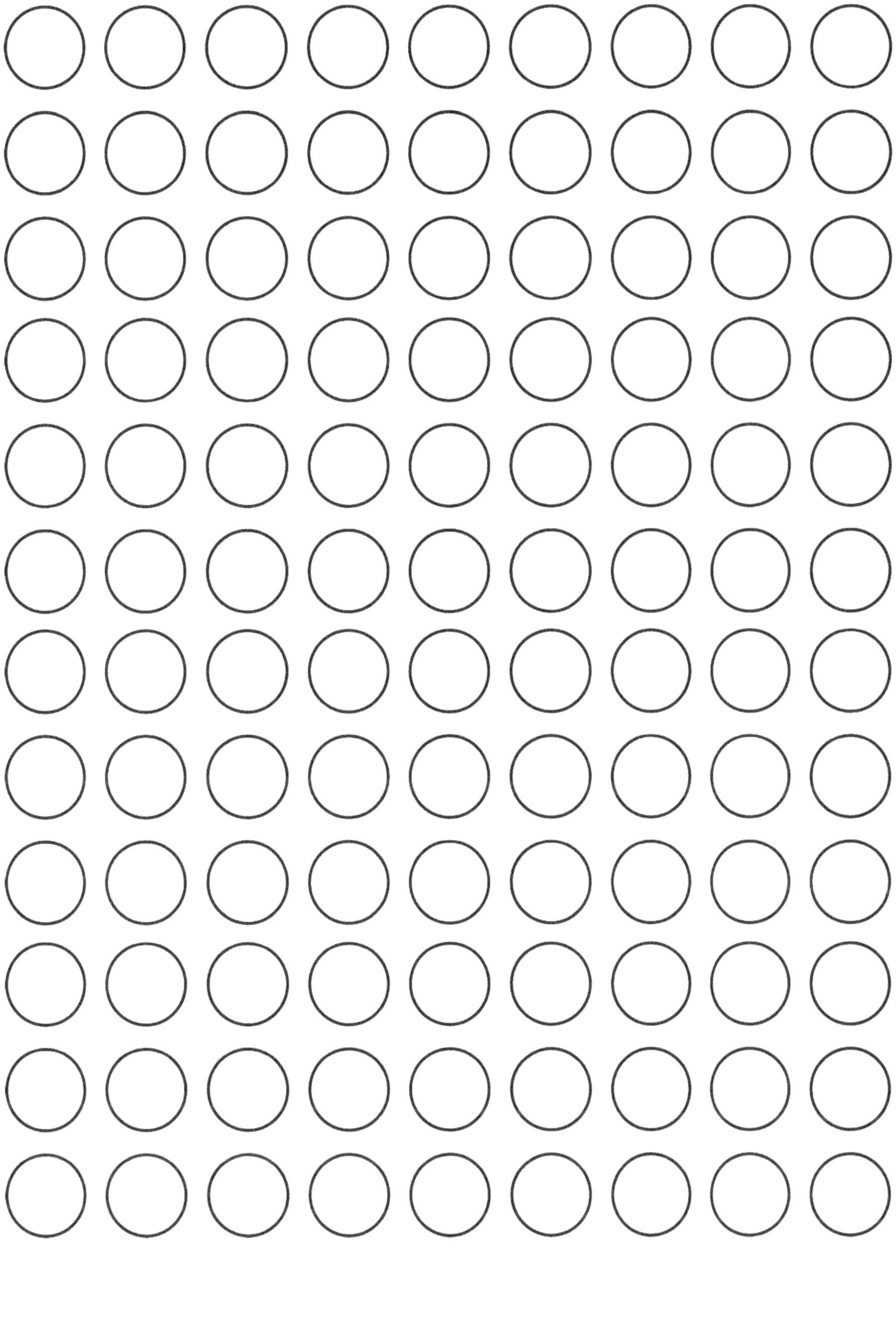

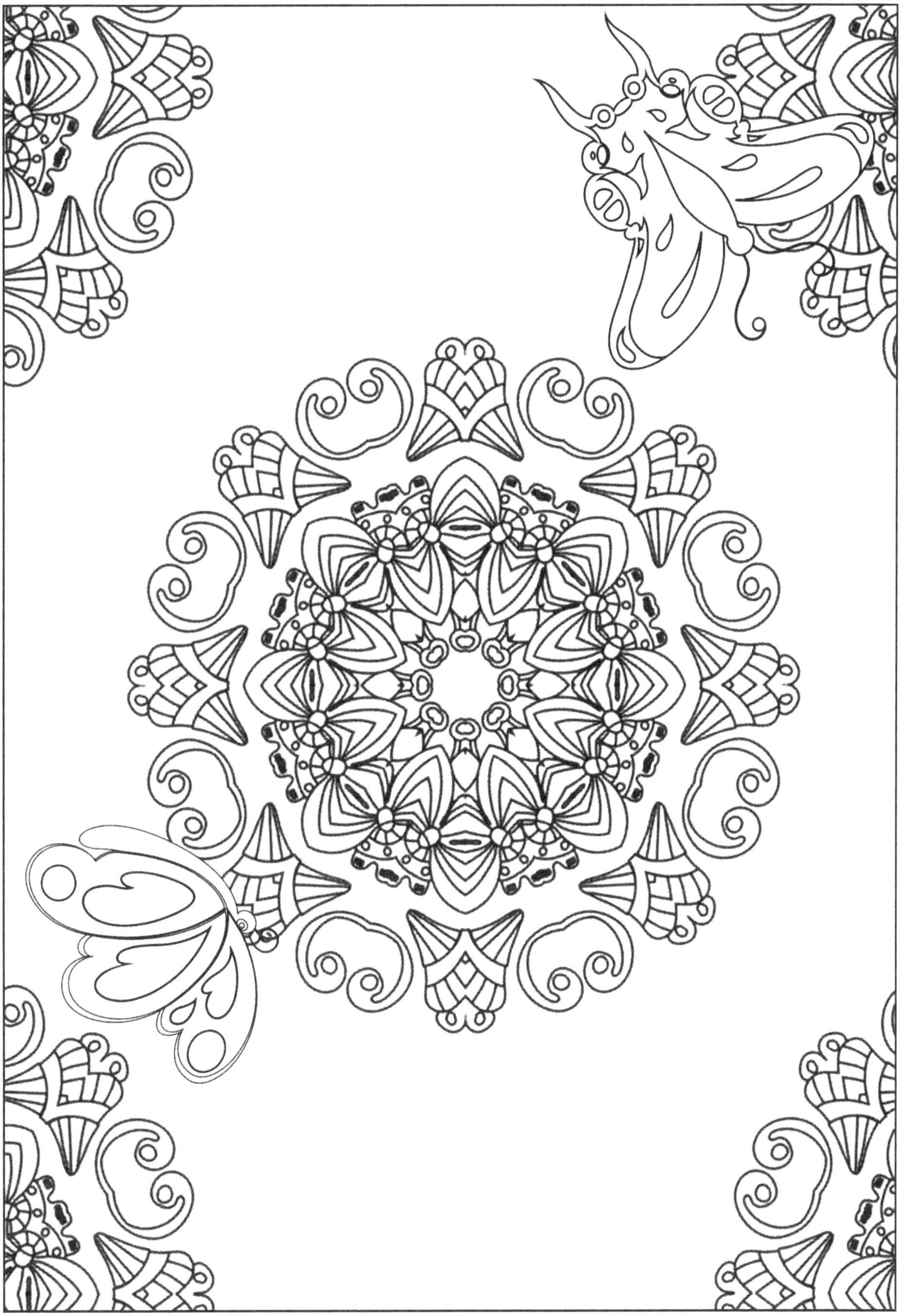

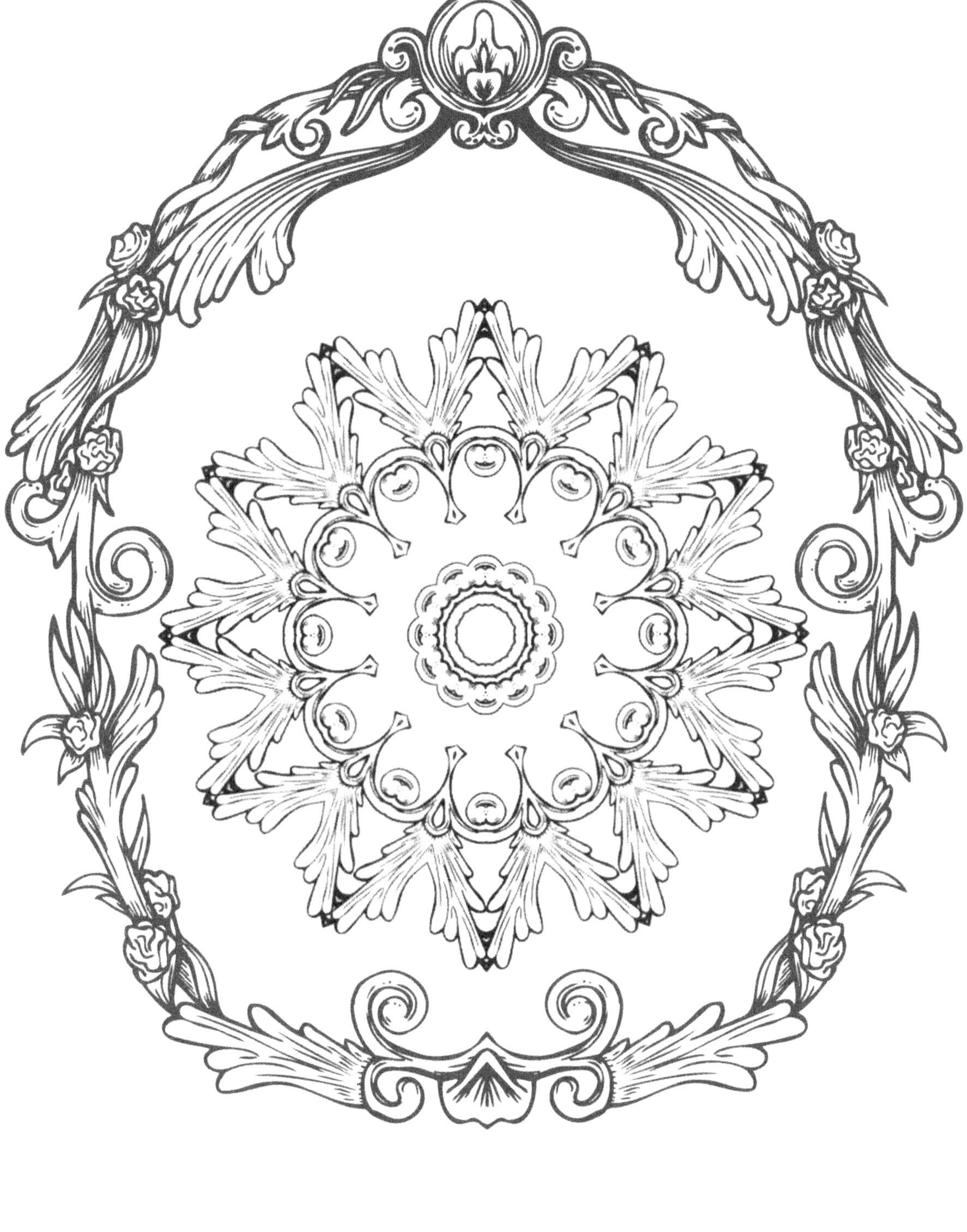

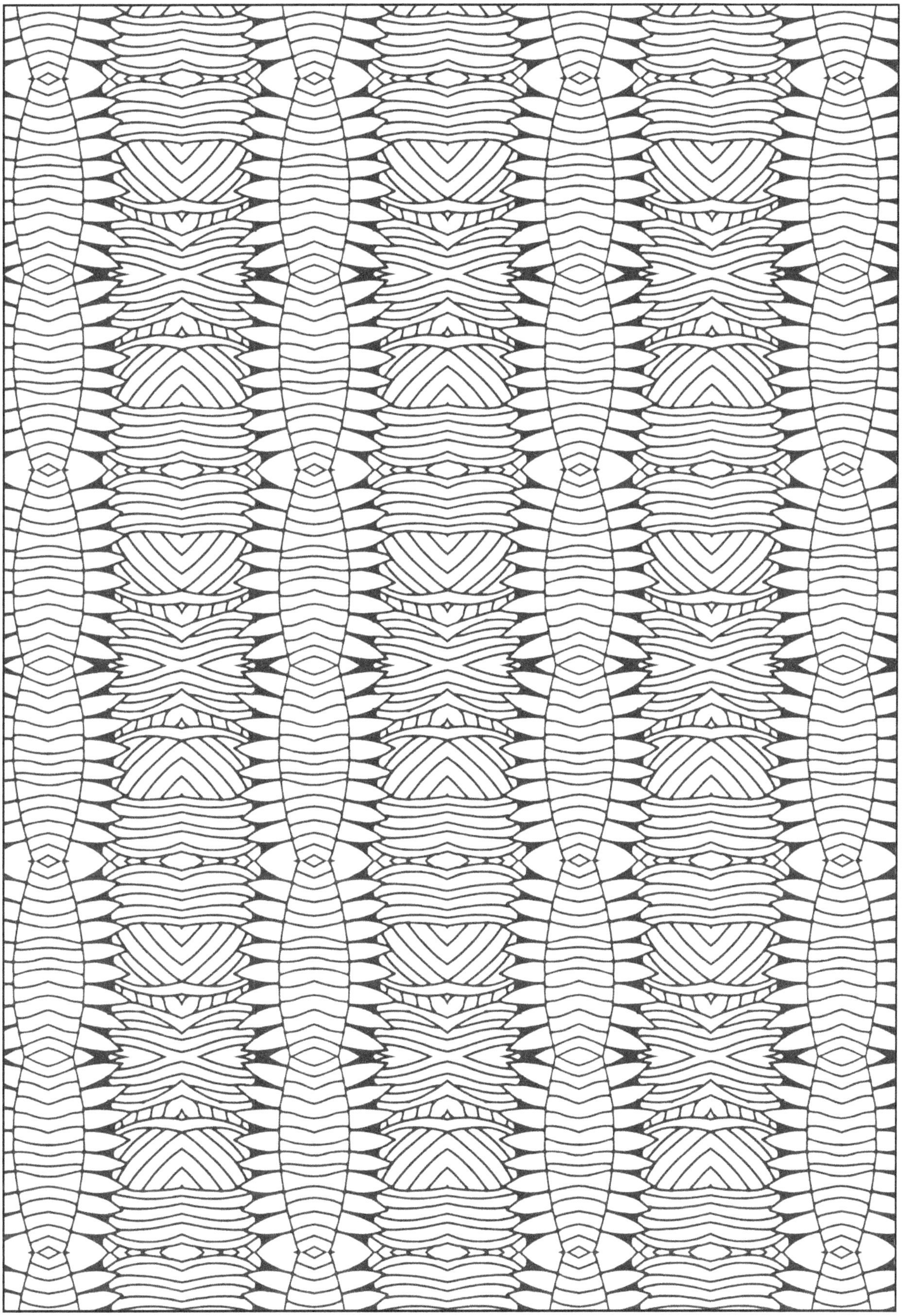

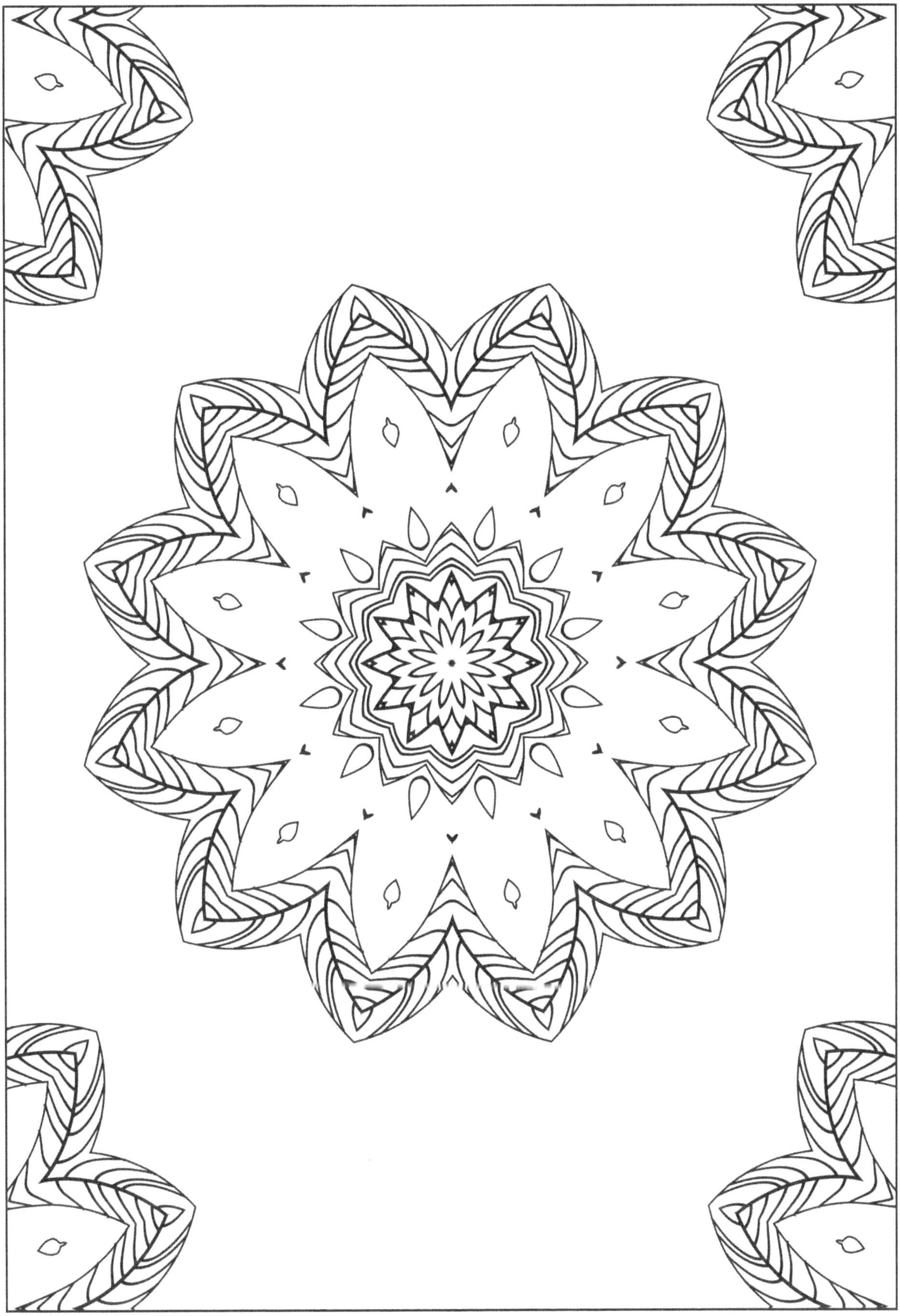

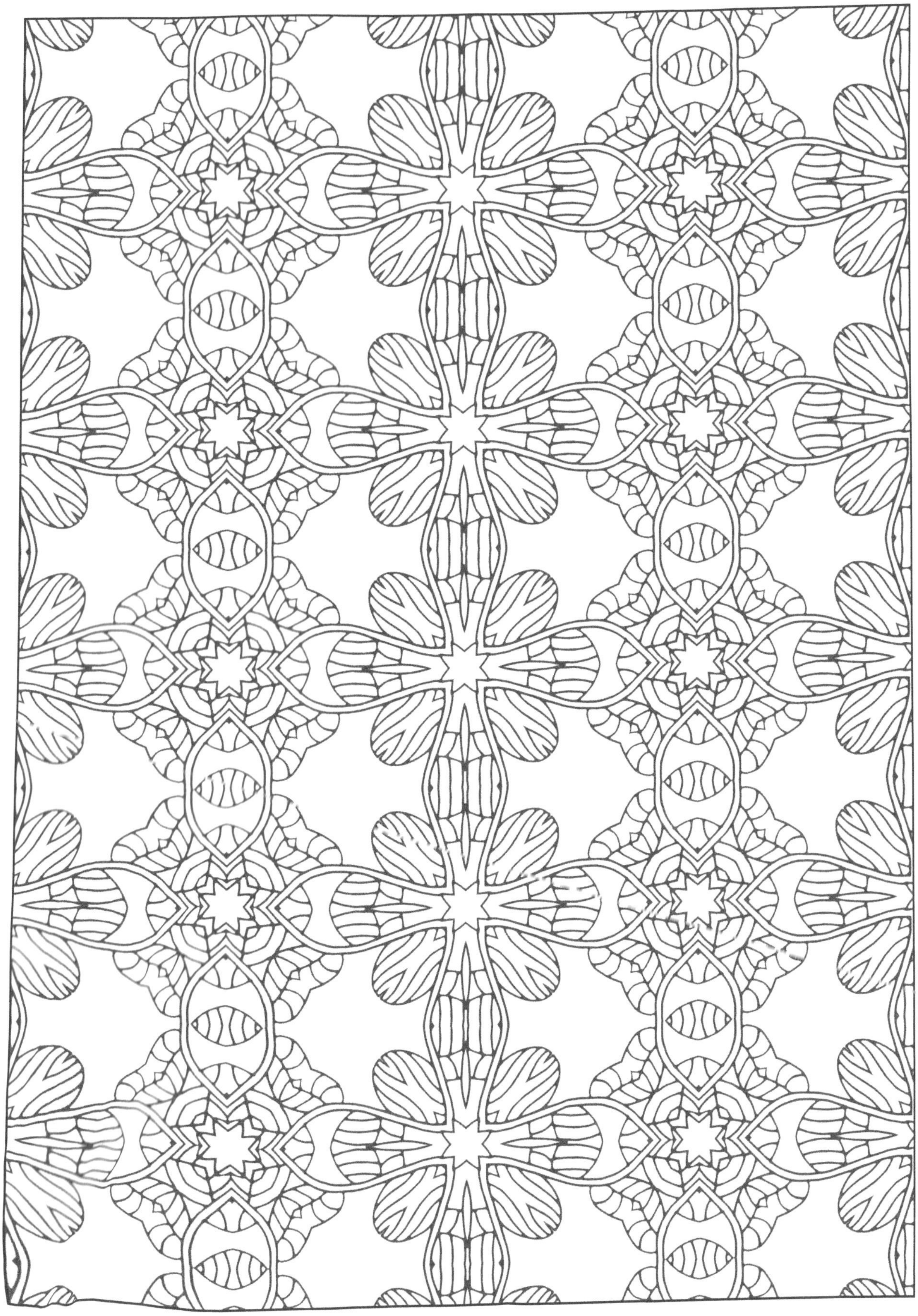

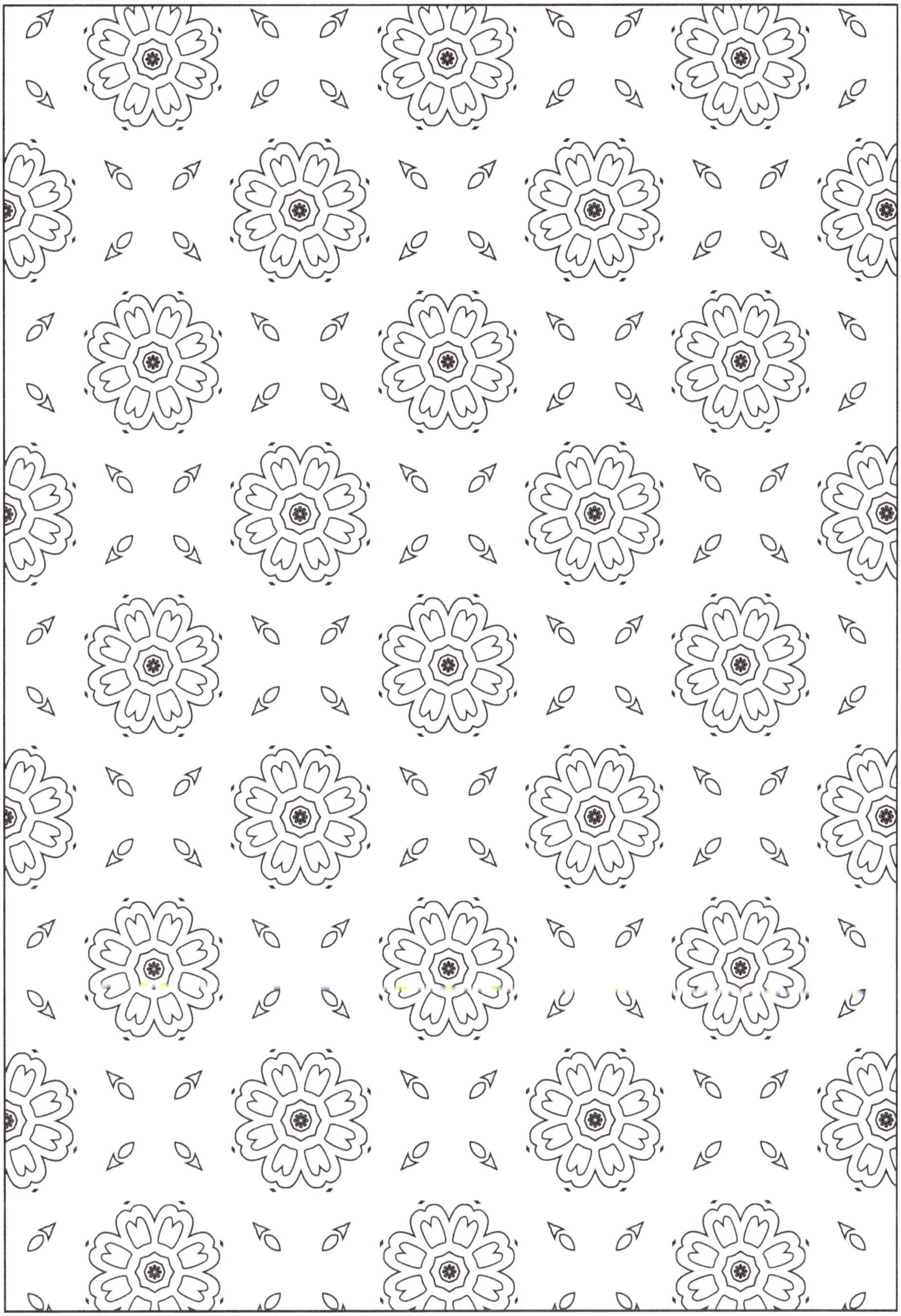

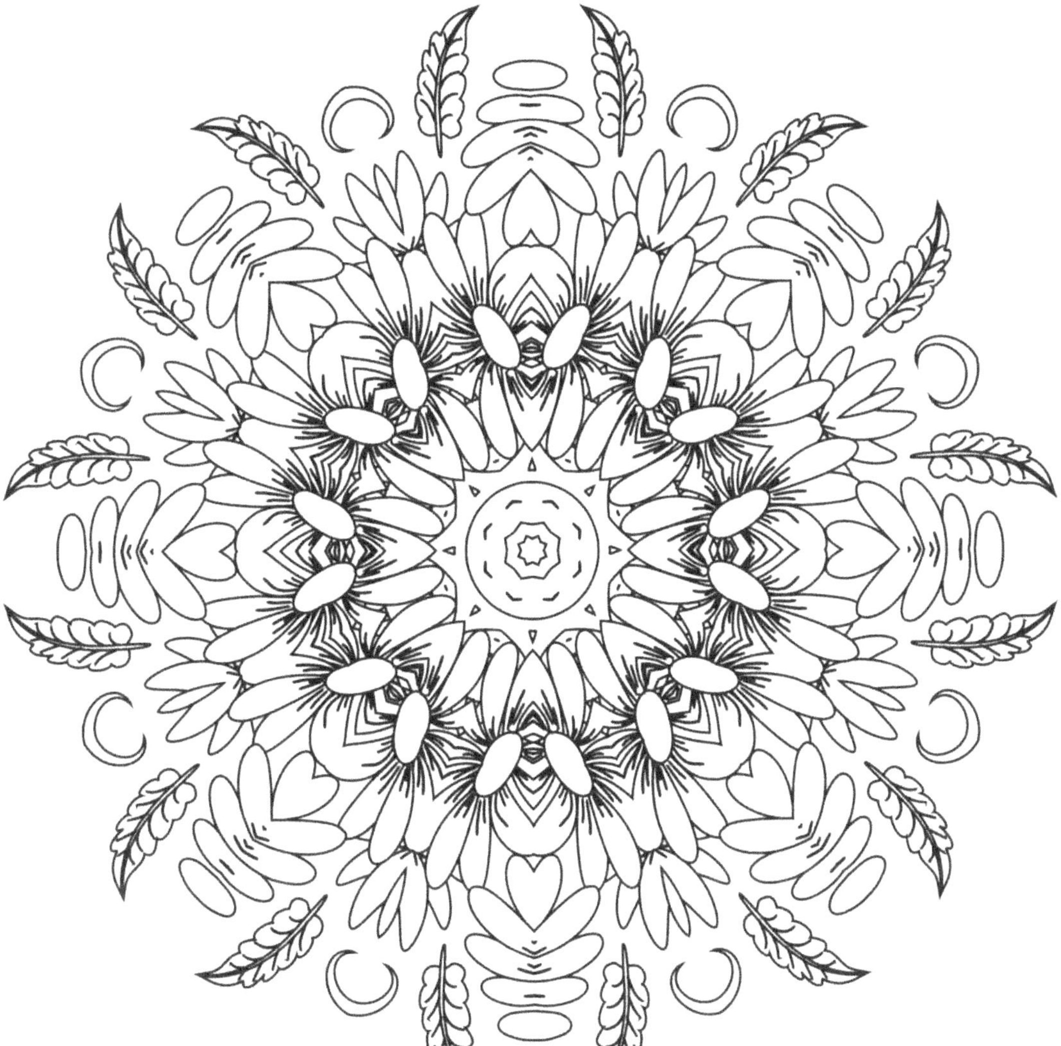

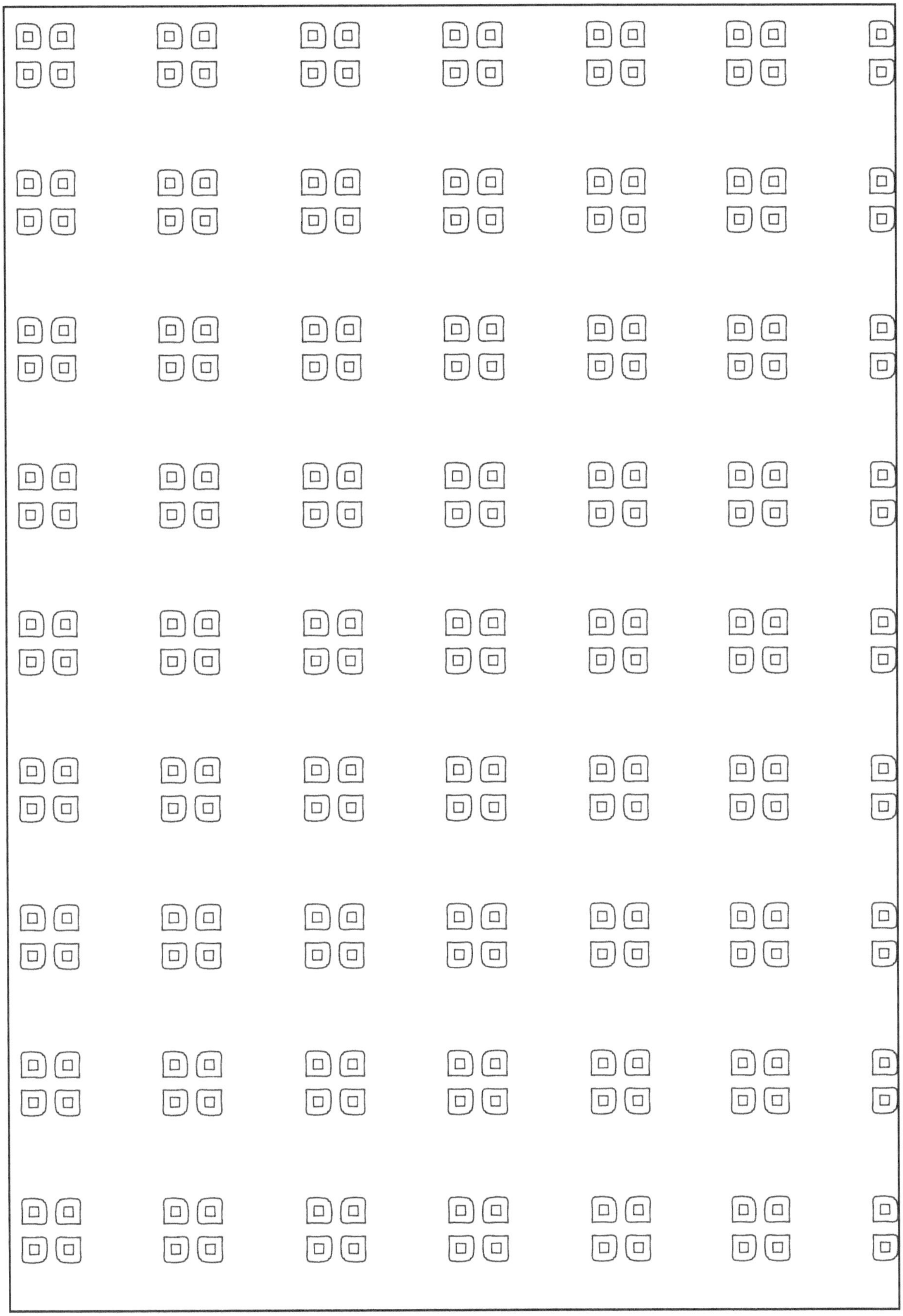

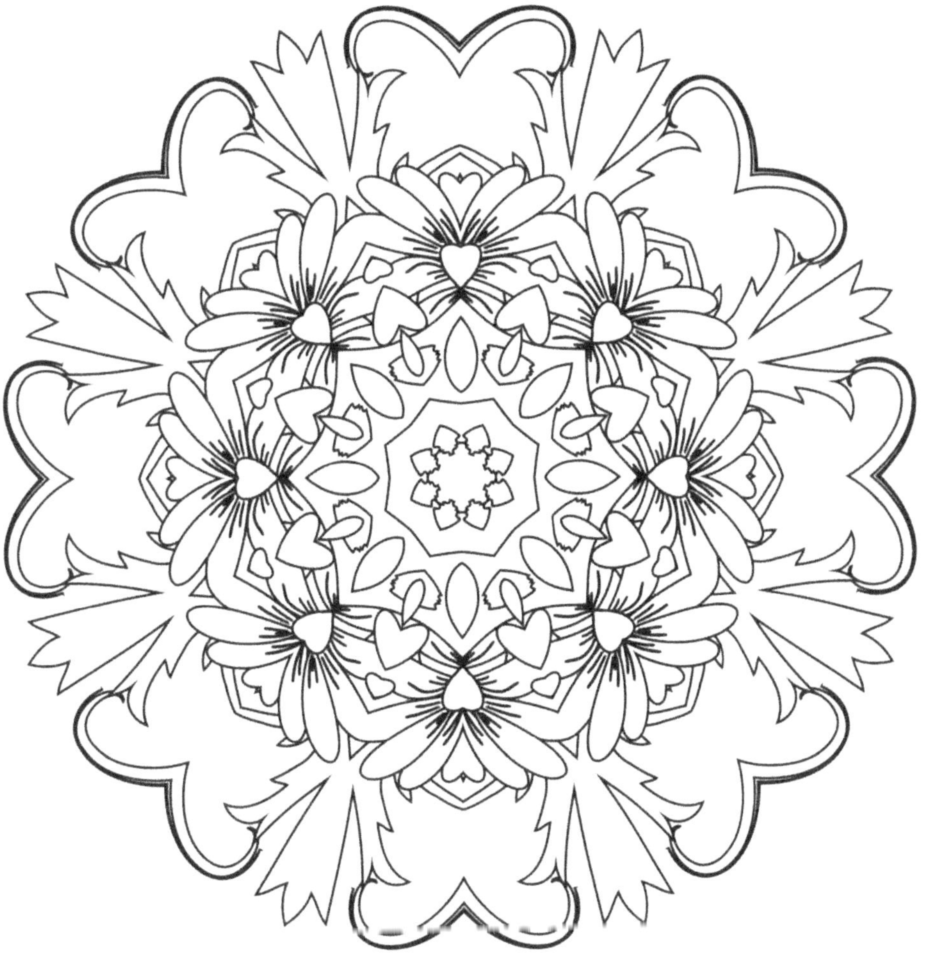

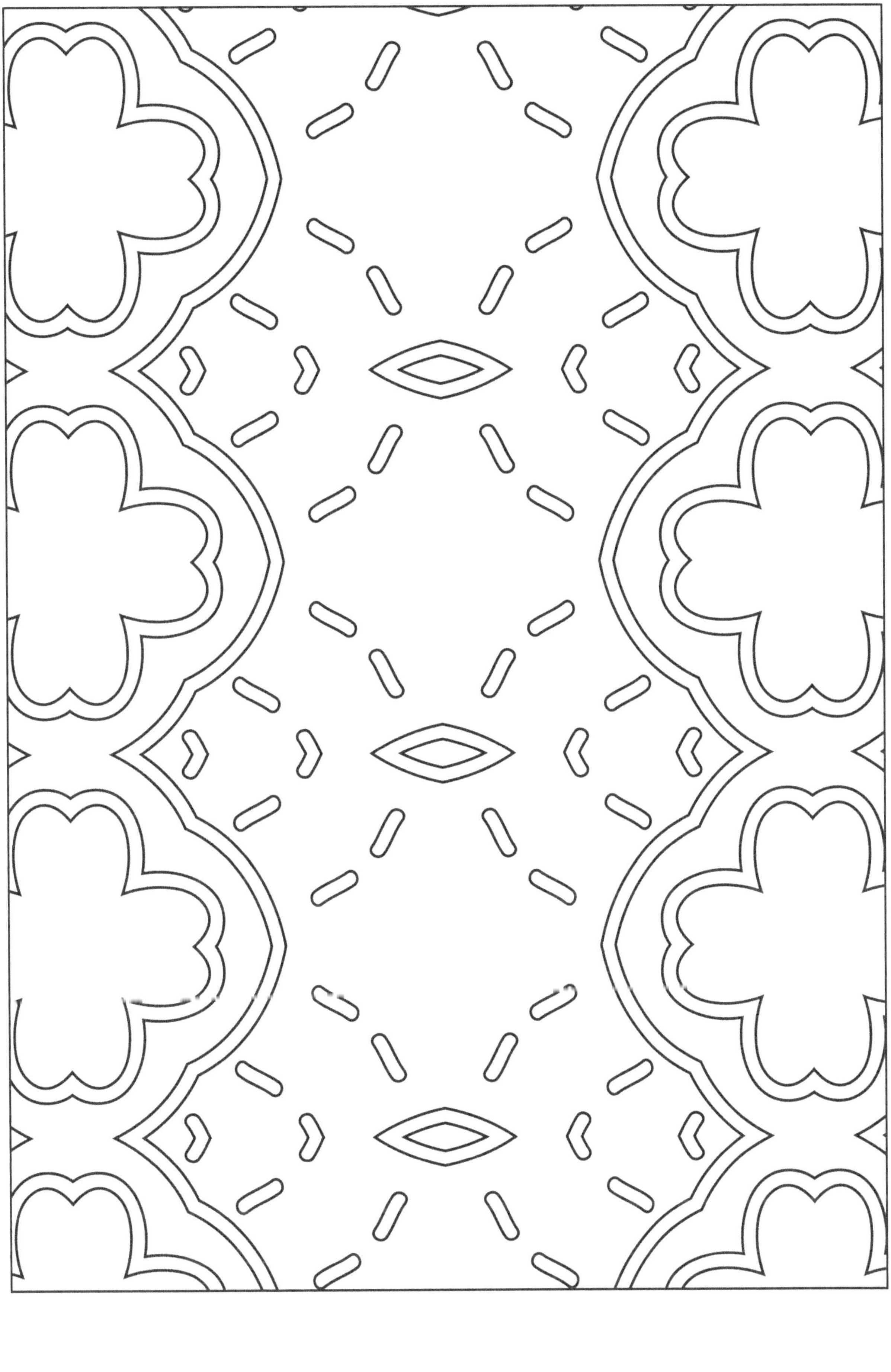

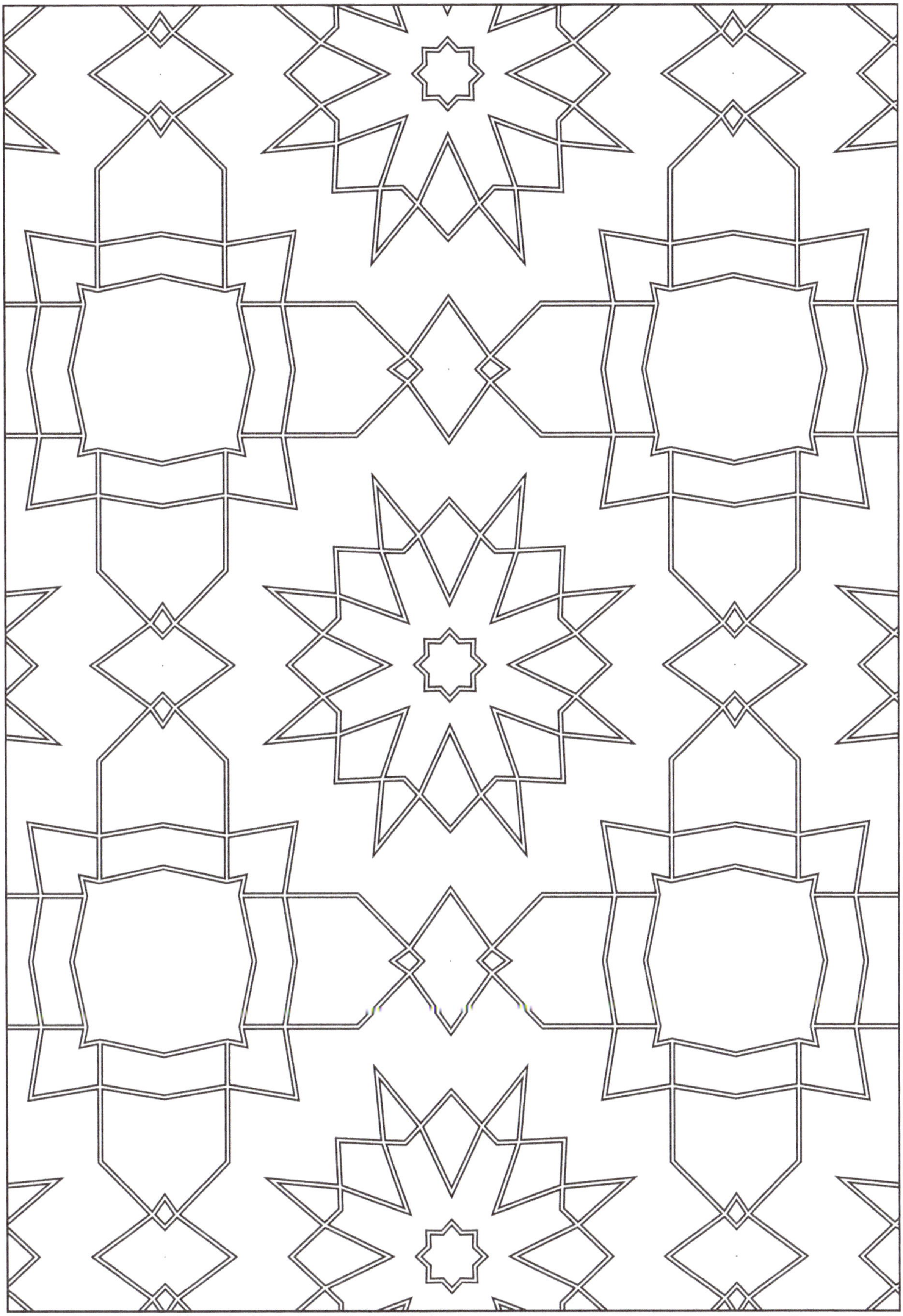

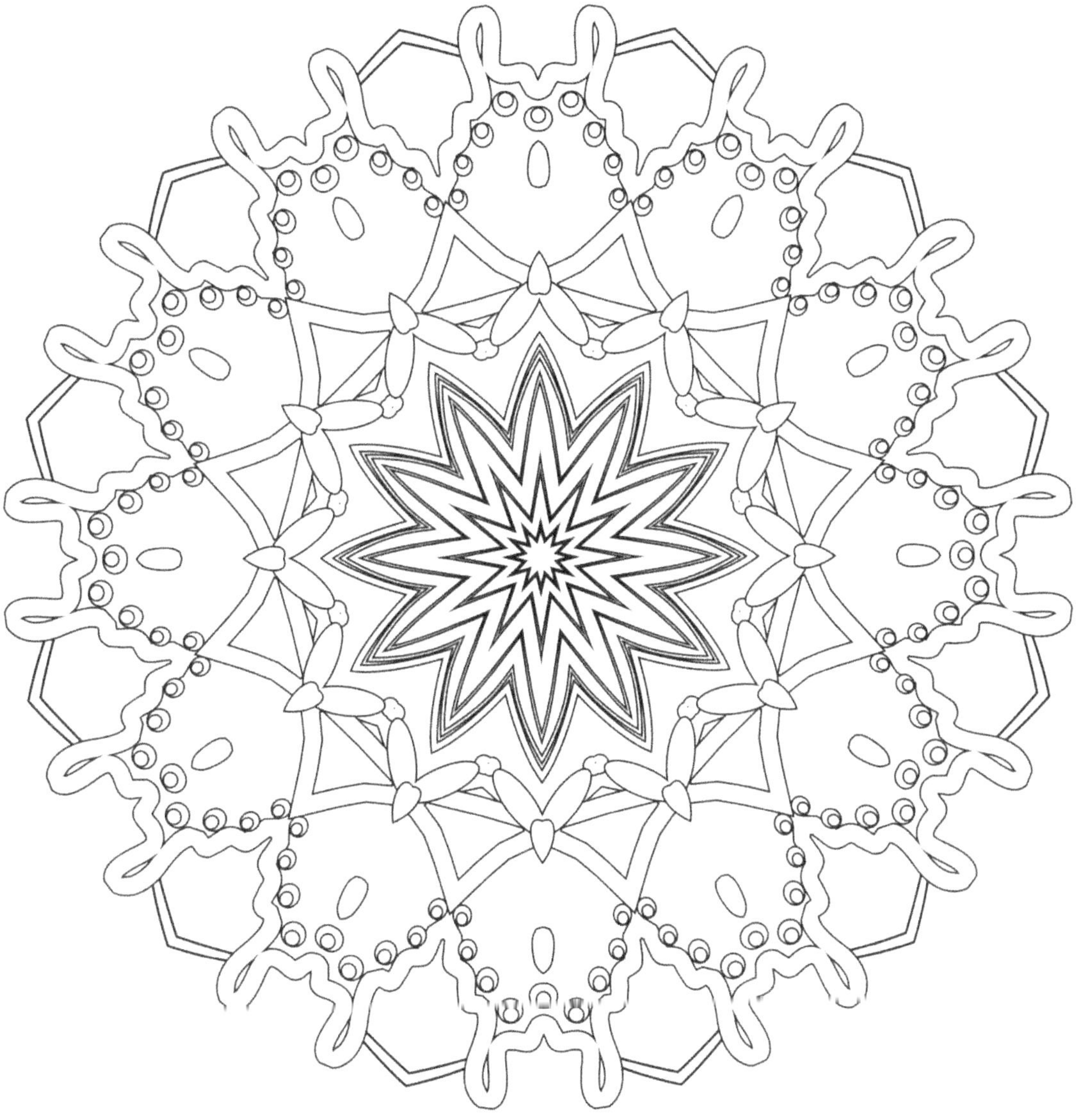

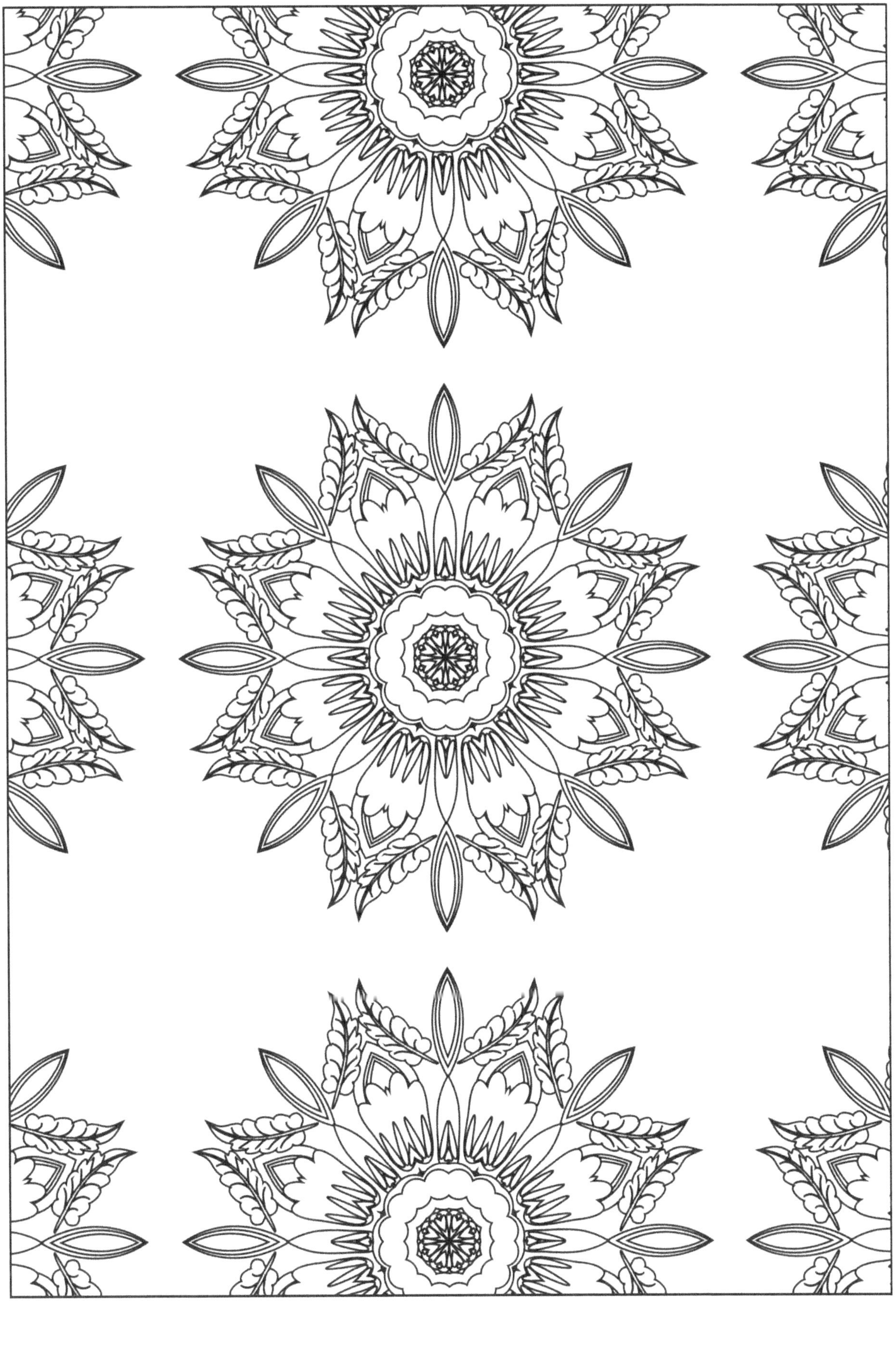

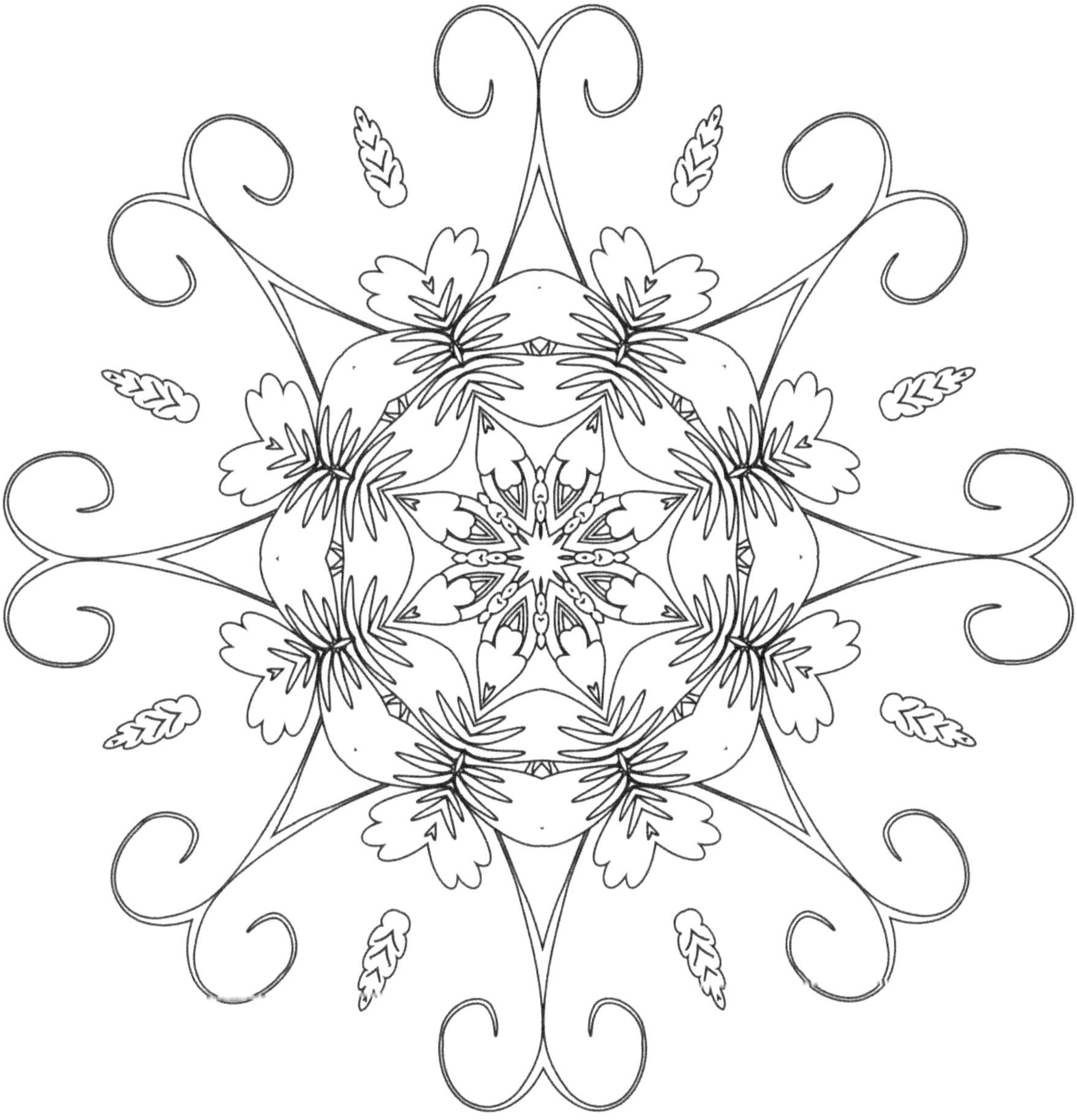

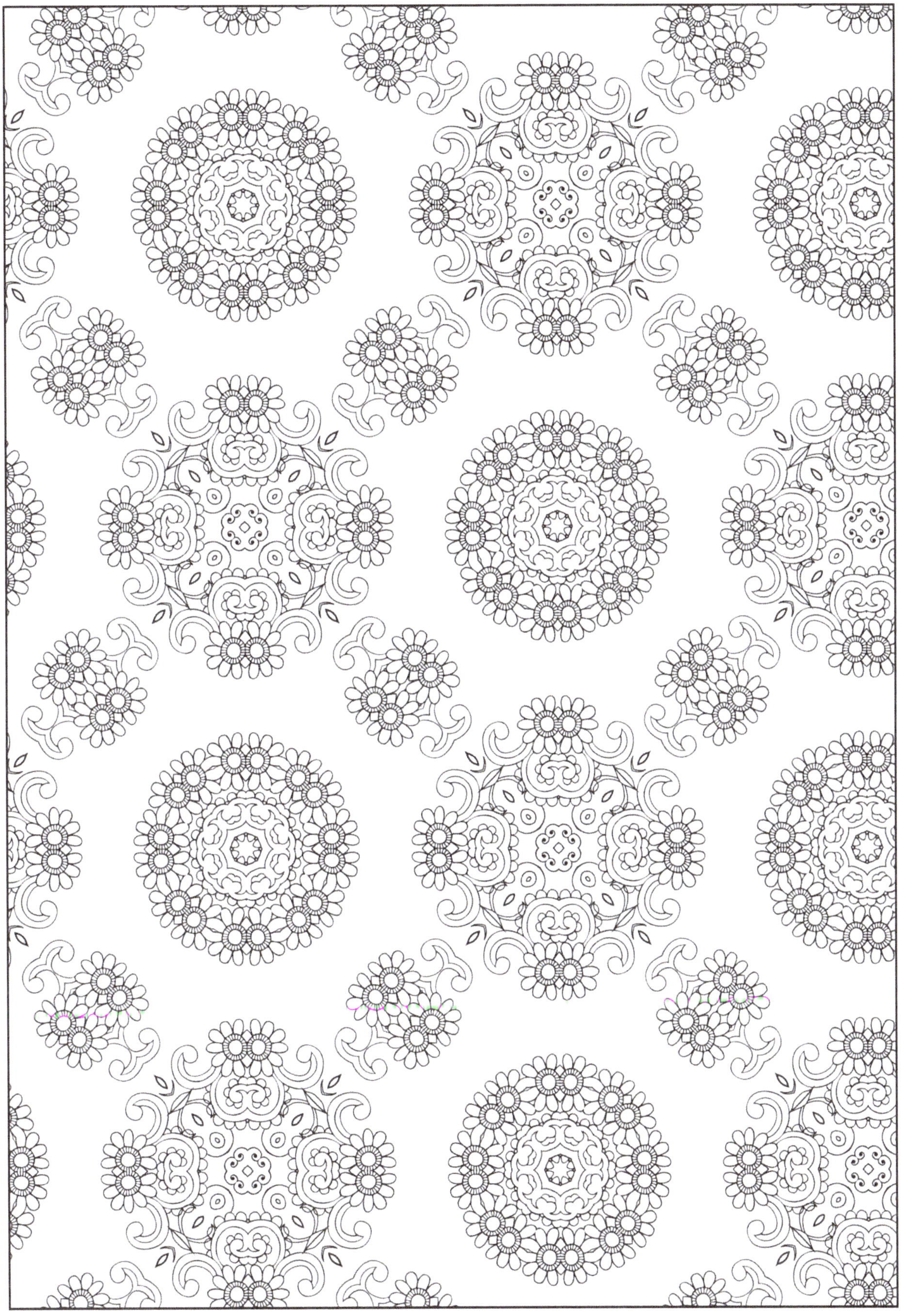

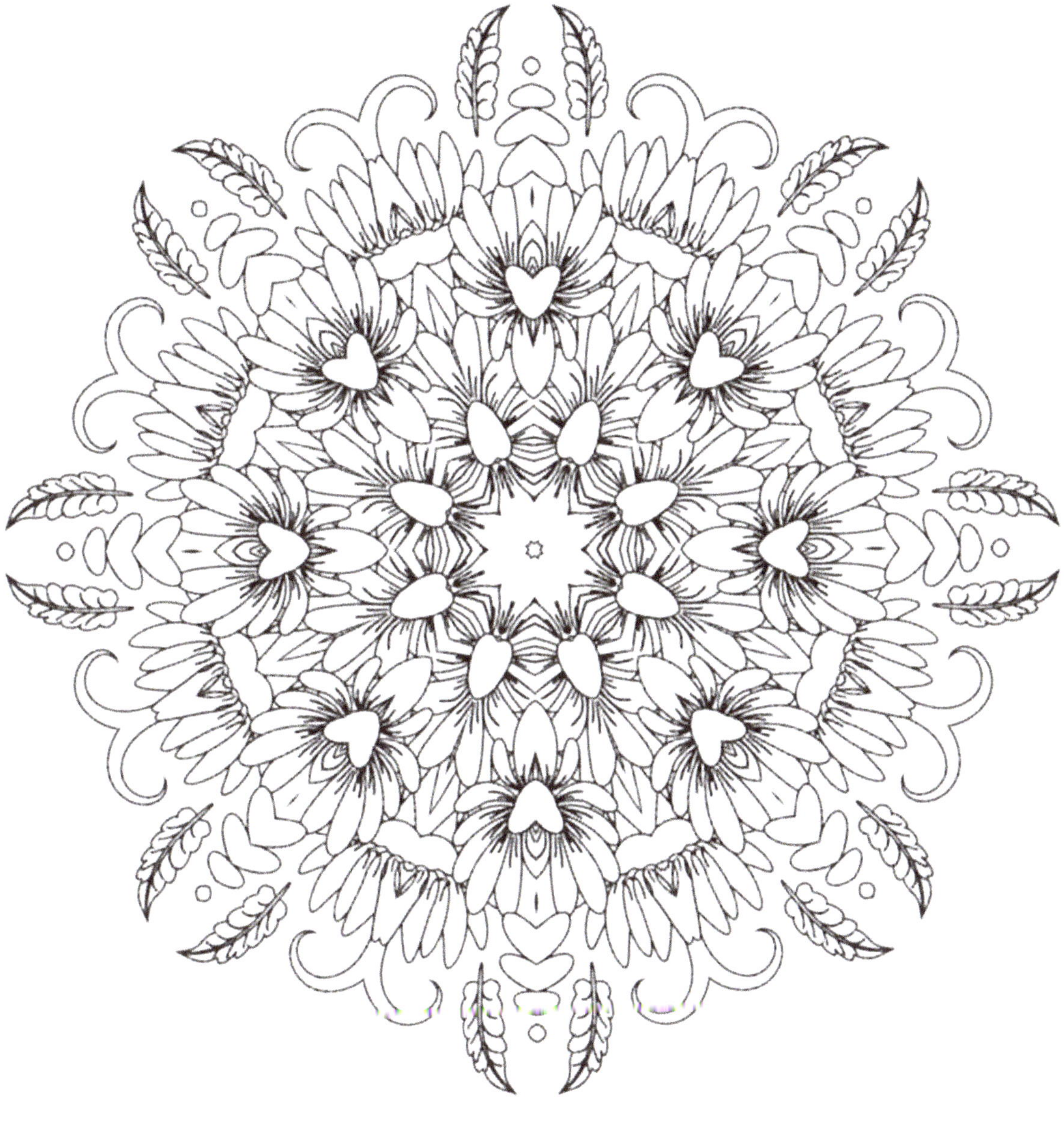

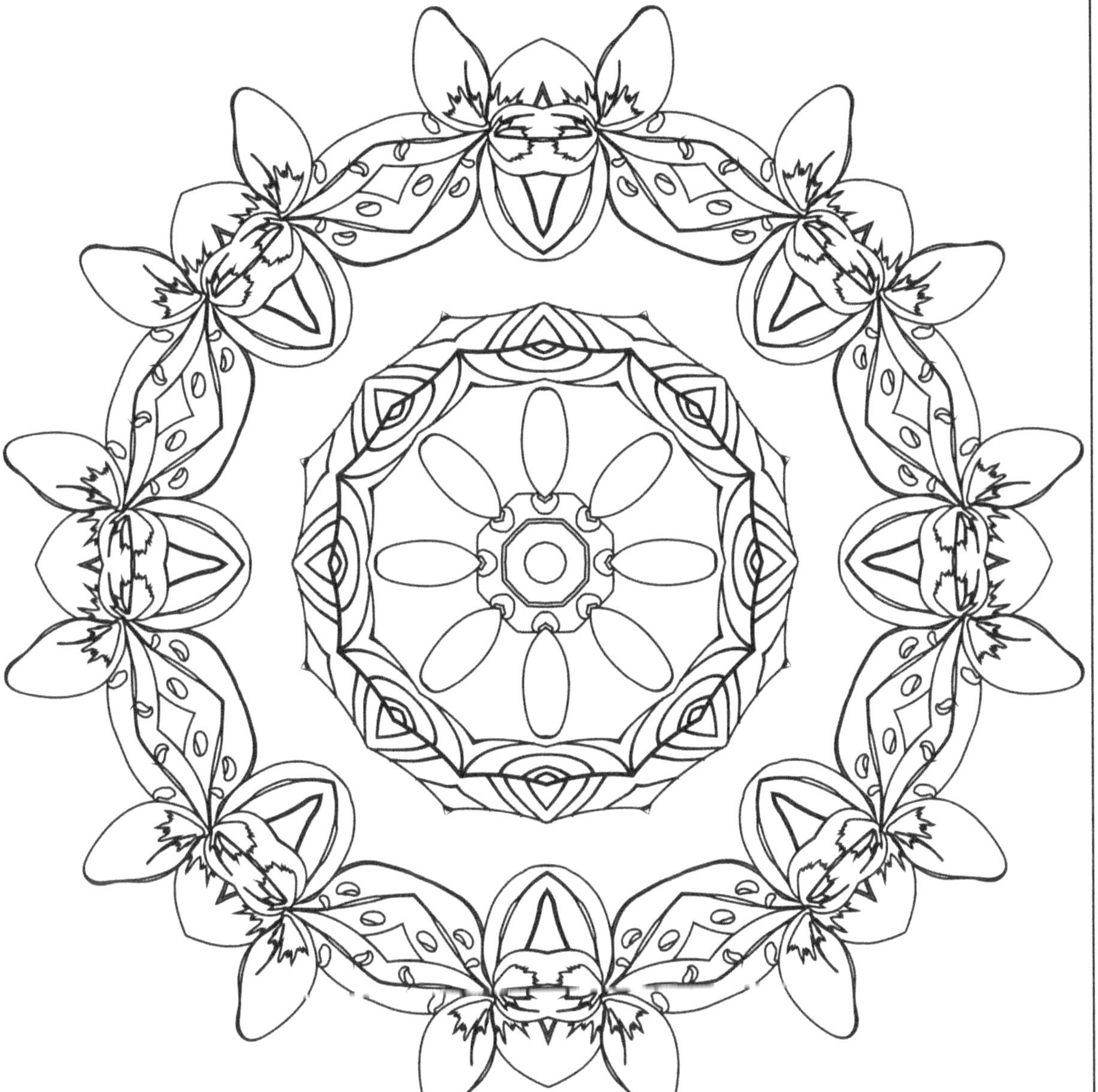

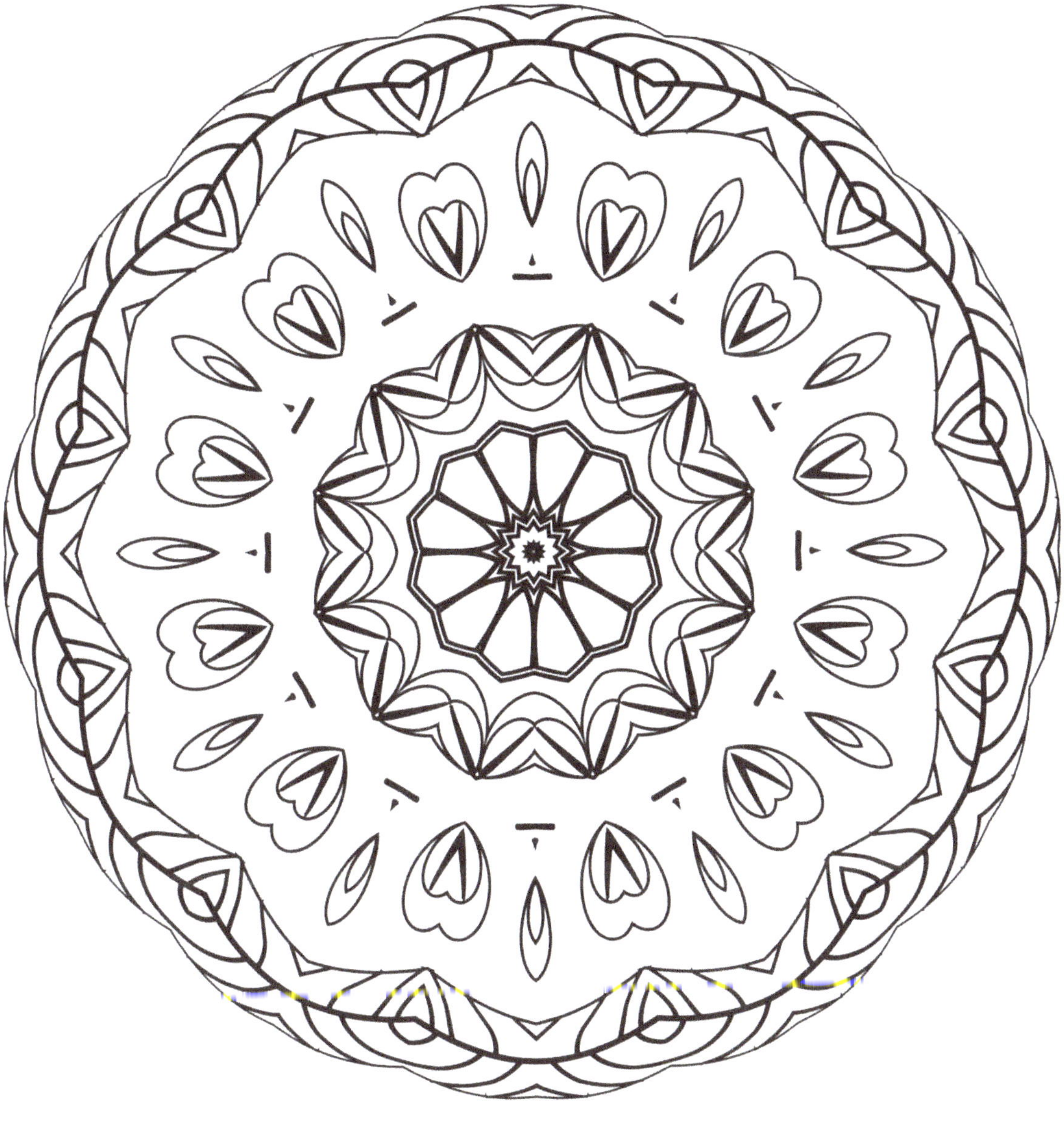

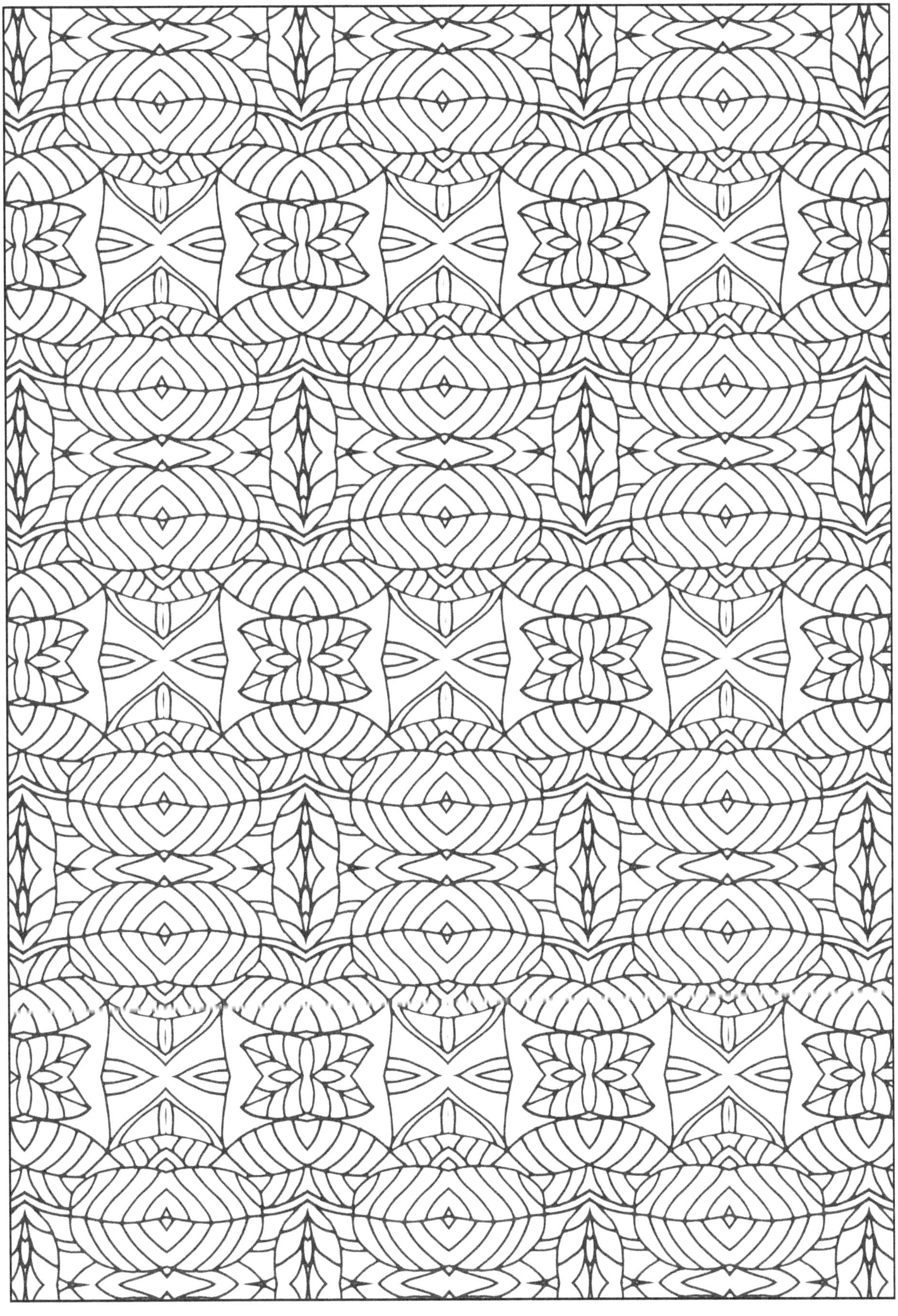

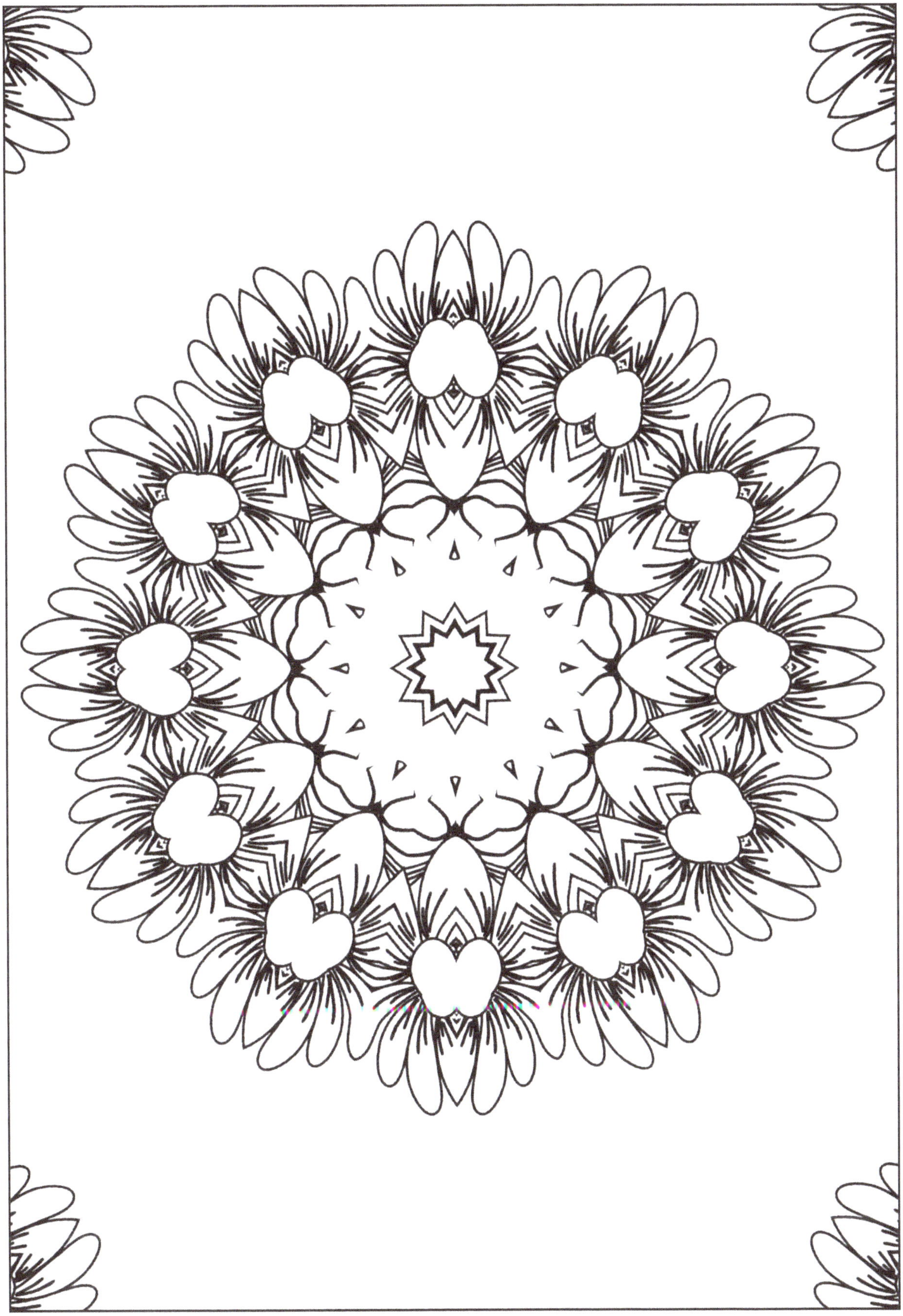

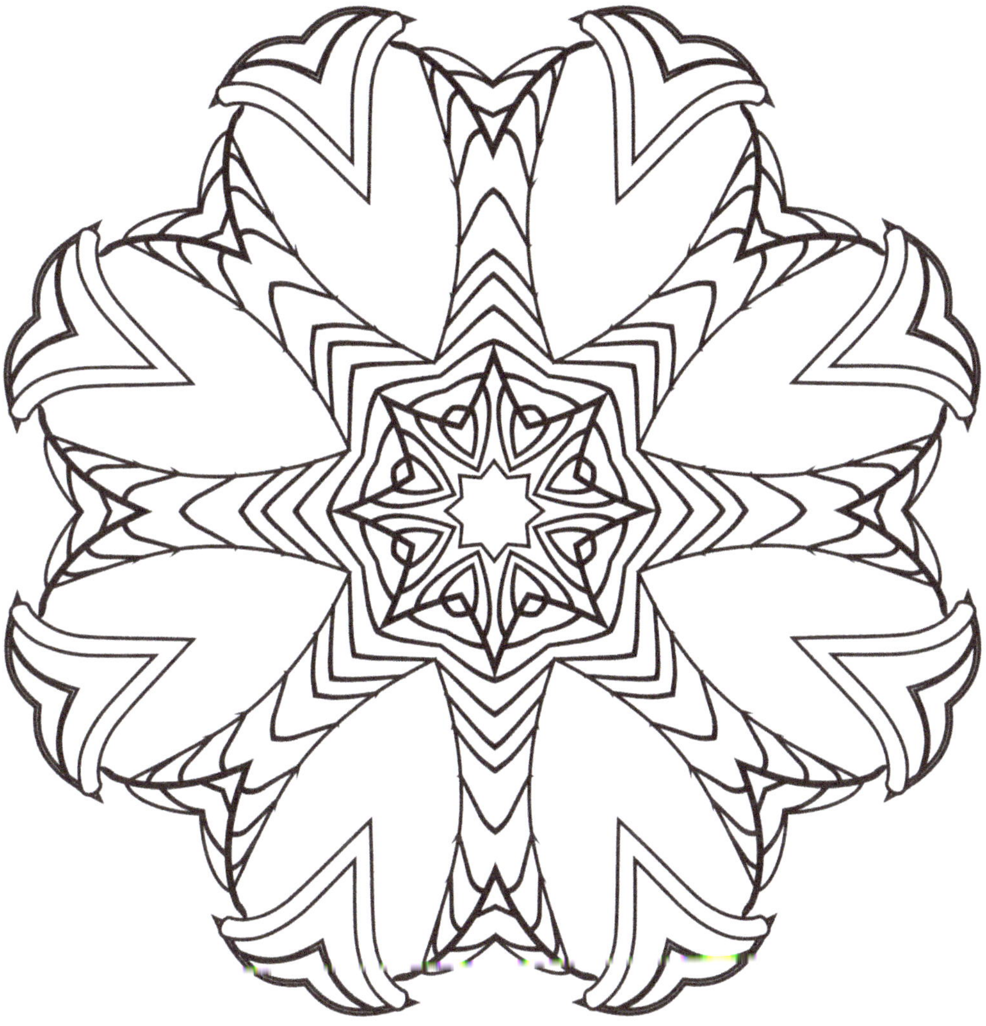

www.ingramcontent.com/pod-product-compliance
Lightning Source LLC
Chambersburg PA
CBHW081753280526
45789CB00008B/2836
9781539380078